MW01292032

Gypsy Fortune Telling with Playing Cards –

How to Read Ordinary Playing Cards like an Expert

Carole Somerville

ISBN-13: 978-1500316730
ISBN-10: 1500316733

Just like the tarot, ordinary playing cards can be used to give insight into a person's life and personality and a glimpse into the future. There are many theories about the history of cartomancy but it is thought that the Gypsies who left their native lands to roam introduced fortune-telling cards to Europe in the fifteenth century. The 52-card deck originally came from the 78-card tarot deck and although today many gypsies read the Tarot, some Romani families still keep up the old tradition of reading ordinary playing cards.

As with tarot there are many different ways to interpret the cards and this book contains a range of easy to understand methods for reading ordinary playing cards with detailed meanings for each card. Here you will find all you need to know about cartomancy and before you know it you will be amazing your family friends with your accurate readings.

Contents:

Introduction

Introduction

Although we usually associate psychic readings with tarot cards, not everyone owns a tarot pack. Reading tarot or playing cards can be learned ... it helps to be psychic but you don't have to be to read the cards. A good alternative to tarot cards is the ordinary playing card. Gypsies have used cards to tell fortunes for as far back as can be remembered and it is widely believed that it was the gypsies, travelling from place to place, who first introduced cards to the West.

There are fifty-two playing cards, each with its own traditional meaning and although this guide will provide all the information you need to acquire a basic knowledge of card reading, you will no doubt find that the more you use this method of divination, the more you will build up your own interpretations around each card.

So, you don't have to be psychic, or the seventh child of a seventh child to read the cards. The aim here, is to introduce you to the principles of card reading so that before you know it, you will be reading your own and your friends' and family's fortunes.

There is nothing complicated or too difficult about this book. It has been kept simple and easy to understand. There are several methods of playing card divination included. Some draw on the meanings of the individual cards and others use only numbers or the four suits. Also included are some very simple techniques for quick readings, in-depth meanings of each card and example interpretations that will soon have you giving detailed card readings like an expert.

YOUR PACK OF CARDS

All you need to start reading fortunes is an ordinary deck of playing cards. Treat the pack you use to do your readings with respect. Keep it specifically for the one purpose and don't use it to play games. These cards will be special to you and should be only used for reading. It is important to protect them from outside influences and vibrations.

There are many similarities between playing cards and the tarot deck. They each have four suits with cards numbered one to ten, and each has court cards associated with each suit. The tarot is more colourful and pictorial. Playing cards are fewer in number and do not have the Major Arcana, but this does not, in any way, limit their usefulness in divination.

YOUR FUTURE IN THE CARDS

Before starting on your reading, it must be remembered that the interpretations given in this book are only keys which are intended to set your imagination to work. The more you practise, the more you will come to relate certain events, situations, people and feelings to each card.

It is important to take your card reading seriously and it's worth committing the meanings of each card to memory in order to gain the confidence of your querent (the person for whom you are doing the readings).

As you read the cards, let your imagination and intuition flow. You might find symbols, words or messages coming to you and if so, say these out loud. Don't be afraid to give your own interpretation of the spread. Although each card has an individual meaning, it should be looked at in relation to the other cards in a spread. Remember that you are the one who is doing the card reading. – Trust your intuition.

How often should you do a reading? There's an old saying that the cards get tired and you might find that you have to limit your readings to a certain number each day. Also, if you feel that the mood is wrong or that the cards just aren't speaking to you on a particular day, don't force anything to come to you. Ask your sitter to come back another day.

It's also important to note that people do take these predictions seriously. When reading other people's cards, you are in a very responsible position. There is a need, therefore, to be diplomatic if the spread looks to be overly gloomy. The person is obviously going through a difficult time and you won't want to make them feel worse by highlighting this. There are always positives in the negatives, and it's your job to look for these!

(i) The Suits and Numbers

In order to understand the nature of the cards, we will start with the suits. Once you understand the associations and qualities of the four suits this will help you form an impression of the basic feel of a spread. What, for instance, might it mean to have a predominance of Spades? What might be expected if most cards in the spread are Diamonds?

If there is a balance of suits, the cards will not focus on one specific area but instead will cover various aspects of life depending on the actual cards and which position in the spread they happen to fall in. (Preparation for and spread layouts will be discussed later).

The Suits

The suits can be related to the astrological elements: Fire, Earth, Air and Water.

Hearts

The Hearts suit, as its symbol suggests, relates to matters of the heart: love, romance, hope, anticipation, happiness and joy, emotional loss and disappointment (heart-ache).To love, there must be partnership, companionship and affection. Hearts will therefore relate to friends, loved-ones and family. As in life, there is good and bad, happy and sad, positive and negative and the cards too will reflect this. How you work out the plusses and minuses within a reading will also be discussed later.

So the hearts: what do you see in the heart suit? What should you be thinking? Hearts relate to people who are close to the querent: their partner, relatives, housemates, old friends and new friendships being formed.

Hearts are loving, friendly and giving but this suit can also be selfish, overbearing and demanding.

Hearts are associated with Water element in astrology. This element adds creativity to the romantic hearts as well as passion and inspiration. Heart cards are naturally creative. These cards indicate passion and feeling in whichever area of life they might represent in a reading.

Season represented by the Hearts: Spring

Hearts can be linked to the cup cards in the tarot.

Clubs

Life is an educational journey and Clubs relate to lessons learned on this journey. We learn through developing skills that help us survive in life and build a career. We learn through our interactions with others, through formal education at school, college and university, through training related to our careers and through travel. Every day can be a learning experience and how people benefit from what they learn can be shown by the Clubs. Will they, for instance learn from their mistakes or do they keep repeating the same mistakes over and over?

Clubs are associated with the Sun in astrology, indicating possible new starts/creations, the spark of life itself.

Season represented by the Clubs: Summer

Clubs can be linked to the wand cards of the tarot.

Diamonds

Diamonds deal with the material world and are therefore linked with the Earth element in astrology. Diamonds point to money making ability, material possessions, gifts that are given and received. But the material isn't all about acquisition of wealth. Within the Diamond suit is all that is associated with Mother Nature: the outdoors, the earth, food and natural products, the countryside and practical skills such as carpentry, building, sewing, handicrafts, cooking and gardening.

Season represented by the diamonds is: Autumn

Diamonds can be linked to the pentacle cards of the tarot.

Spades

Spades are associated with the Air element in astrology and are linked with matters of mind, thoughts, ideas, communication and learning. Spades can therefore be linked to the written word, spoken word and body language. Spades draw attention to emails, internet networking sites and text messages as well as letters and documents.

This is the suit that can correspond with the emotions we go through in life but whereas the hearts (red) can represent happiness and joy as well as disappointment, spades (black) mostly deal with negative emotions: uncertainty, upset, fear and anxiety, worry and anger.

Spades are dark cards in that the experiences they relate to can touch the soul. Spades correspond to the winter season when the land lies bare and barren. This suit can be associated with endings and closure and times of preparation/waiting as in the waiting chapter of winter in preparation for rebirth in the spring.

Spades are linked with limitation, restraint, discipline, patience, the necessity for hard work and perseverance. This suit can also be associated with the planet Saturn in astrology.
Season represented by the Spades: Winter
Spades can be linked to the sword cards of the tarot.

Choosing a Significator

Some spreads will need a 'significator', a card to represent the person for whom the reading is being given. The qualities and the personal attributes represented by each suit are as follows:

Hearts are associated with life and emotions; happiness and friendship; romance and marriage; children and creativity.
  As a Significator:
  would represent someone with light brown or auburn hair, blue, grey or hazel eyes.

Clubs are associated with enterprise and initiative; work and ambitions; new activity.
  As a Significator:
  would represent someone with red or brown hair, hazel eyes; an enthusiastic and energetic personality.

Diamonds are associated with money, luck and good fortune; material possessions and earning ability.
  As a Significator:
  would represent someone with fair or greying hair, light blue eyes.

Spades are associated with limitation, obstacles, mental pursuits, communication and misfortune.
  As a Significator:
  would represent someone with dark brown or black hair, dark eyes. A strong character. Someone who is not known to be demonstrative or emotional.

Once you have decided on the representative suit, it is traditional to choose a court card of that suit depending on the age and sex of your querent.
  Kings represent mature men.
  Queens represent mature women.
  Jacks represent youths of either sex.

NUMBERS

When you are reading the cards in a spread it can help to consider the actual numbers on the cards. Before looking at individual cards, think about the association of the numbers and how these might relate to the different suits.

In astrology the numbers can be linked to the Cardinal, Fixed and Mutable signs.

Cardinal cards are active, assertive, energise and spark activity.

Fixed cards stabilise, concentrate and focus on specific areas. These numbers solidify, get results through sticking it out and can be stubborn or unmovable when referring to temperament. Can be stuck in a rut or obsessed too long in one situation depending on the suit and placement in a spread.

Mutable cards can relate to adjustments, adaptability, necessary change and versatility.

Cardinal: Ace (Aries), 4 (Cancer), 7 (Libra) and 10 (Capricorn)

Fixed: 2 (Taurus), 5 (Leo), 8 (Scorpio) and 11 (Aquarius)

Mutable: 3 (Gemini), 6 (Virgo), 9 (Sagittarius) and 12 (Pisces)

ASSOCIATION OF NUMBERS

Each number on a card has a basic meaning of its own and it can help to learn these. Remember that as in all methods of divination, you should go with your intuition. Nothing is written in stone and a meaning that feels right for one person may not feel right for another. All interpretations in this book are purely suggestions and when you start reading regularly you will discover that intuitively you will develop your own meanings for the cards.

Individual Number Meanings:

1 – New Beginnings; new energy; ability to achieve goals

2 – Partnerships; balance; conflict and opposition; compromise, pause

3 – Good fortune; reason to celebrate; trios i.e. past, present and future/beginning, middle and end

4 – Stability; foundations

5 – Change and creativity

6 – Harmony; equality; dependability

7 – Opportunity to take creative or intelligent action
8 – Solidity of the cube (four being solidity of the square); infinity; success; expansion
9 – Attainment; affluences; satisfaction.
10 - Completion

Brief summary of associations with the numbers when reading playing cards:

Card Number	Zodiac sign	Action	Circumstance
1	Aries	Initiate	New beginnings
2	Taurus	Hold back or compromise	A journey, partnership or arrangement just begun. Balance. Opposition.
3	Gemini/Aquarius	Adapt, communicate	Achievement of short-term goals. Communication and connection.
4	Cancer/Pisces	Stabilise	Period of assessment and meditation
5	Leo	Make choices or changes	Continuation of ventures already begun. Disturbance.
6	Virgo	Analyse	Period of review and analysis. Harmony.
7	Libra	Balance	Sorting out priorities and getting life in balance. Regroup. Reassess.
8	Scorpio	Solidify, brings karmic events into play	Build on strengths
9	Sagittarius	Movement	Setting long-term goals. Striking out.
10	Capricorn	Achievement, completion	Celebration

(ii) Spreads

When you do a reading for yourself or someone else, you should set up the table in a way that puts you in the right mood to start reading. You might have a favourite cloth that you keep just for your readings. Spread this on the table. You may want to light some candles or incense and to ask your guides or angels for guidance before doing the readings.

You should shuffle the cards first. Then ask the person you are reading for to shuffle the cards. They should keep shuffling until they feel ready to stop. They should then separate the deck into three piles before stacking the piles back on top of each other in a random order. Once they are happy, they should hand the cards back to you.

You are now ready to lay out the cards in a chosen spread. There are many different spreads you can use. Some are for a specific purpose while others will give a more general reading. This chapter gives suggestions for a variety spreads. You might experiment with different ones and even make up spreads of your own.

Some spreads will not use all the cards in a deck as in the Gypsy Method below. Other spreads will use all cards including the Joker. In-depth meanings of the individual cards will be given in the next chapters.

TRADITIONAL INTERPRETATIONS

There are a number of spreads and a number of ways in which the cards can be read. You might want to try a few of the following ideas to begin with, but you will soon realise which methods work best for you.

GYPSY METHOD

Traditionally, gypsies used thirty-two cards of the pack. They would discard the twos, threes, fours, fives and sixes.

Shuffling and Cutting

Once you have discarded the above cards and you are ready to do your reading, shuffle the remaining pack thoroughly and then hand the cards to your querent. He or she should then shuffle the cards. After this, they should cut the cards by dividing them into three heaps with the left hand, then gather the heaps together, one on top of the other to form a pile in the centre of the table.

How to read the cards in the Gypsy spread

Take the cards and spread them on the table in the shape of a fan. Ask the querent to choose thirteen cards from the fan. Take the remaining cards and put them to one side. Deal out the thirteen cards again into the shape of a fan and you are ready to do your reading.

Before examining the individual cards, you should look to see whether one suit seems to dominate over the others. Does a particular number occur more than once? If so, the significance of these should be explained as this will help give an overall 'feeling' to the spread.

Suits that dominate this spread

If **Hearts** dominate you should emphasise love and romantic issues.

If **Clubs** dominate, work or volunteer matters or everyday responsibilities might be on the sitter's mind.

If **Diamonds** dominate, money and material matters are important.

If **spades** dominate, this could be a sign of disappointment, unhappiness or disillusion.

Numbers that dominate this spread

Aces suggest new beginnings.
Sevens suggest friendships, joint projects and related finances.
Eights suggest long-term financial investments and sexual attraction.
Nines suggest hopes, wishes or possible worries.
Tens suggest travel and emotional matters.
Knaves (or Jacks) suggest young men or women.
Queens suggest the influence of an older woman.
Kings suggest the influence of an older man.

The Reading

You are now ready to consider each card individually (card interpretations are given in the next chapters) but as you do so, you should continually build up a picture in your mind. Start reading the cards from left to right but weave the meanings together, as you proceed from one end of the fan to the other.

The Diamond Spread

Once you get a feel for your cards, you may want to try a different spread. You can choose to use your thirty-two card pack or you may wish to use the whole deck. It is up to you. Meanings or all of the cards are given in this book.

For the Diamond Spread, ask your querent to shuffle and cut the cards twice. Again, spread them in the shape of a fan and ask the querent to select nine cards. Deal these nine cards face up in a diamond shape on the table.

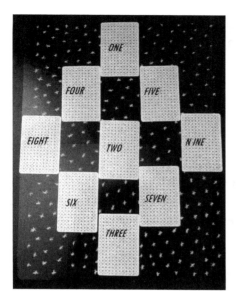

Deal them out in the order in which they are numbered above.

Card One: gives an overall indication and this can be read by considering its suit. A **Heart** in this position suggests success in love; a **Club** – success in education or training; a **Diamond** – luck with money; a **Spade** – possible disappointments ahead, depending on indicators from the rest of the spread.

Card Two: gives indication of when the next important event in life will occur. The higher the number, the longer the wait. The lower the number the closer the sitter is to a turning point in life.

Card Three: gives indication of possible factors which will influence the two previous cards.

Cards Four and Five: indicate sitter's luck. These cards should be read together.

Cards Six and Seven: refer to friendships, charitable interests and social life in general.

Cards Eight and Nine: Indicators of likely events in the near future.

FULL PACK SPREADS

Once you have experimented with using the traditional thirty-two card spread, you might want to try other spreads that use the full pack. One or two further examples will be given but there's no reason why you can't work out your own personal layout.

Layout Example one:

PAST   PRESENT   FUTURE

This is self-explanatory. Deal out three cards and interpret them according to the past, present and future. You might want to place more than one card in each position to give a more detailed reading.

Layout Example Two:

SEVEN CARD SPREAD

Deal out seven cards, one after the other and take each card as representing either the next seven days, or the next seven months. The first card, for example, will represent Day One, the second Day Two, through to Day Seven.

Layout Example Three:

SEVENTEEN CARD SPREAD

This method uses the full pack. Take out the card representing your sitter (significator) and place it on the table. Ask your sitter to shuffle the full pack and cut it twice. Once it has been handed back to you, deal out the cards in the order shown below. This spread relies entirely on the suit that falls in each position and the numbers on the cards are ignored.

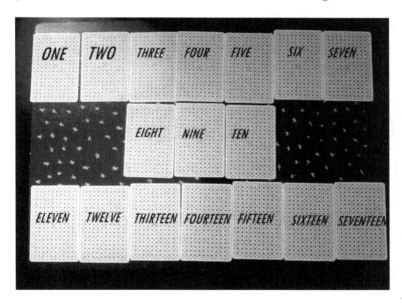

Cards 1 to 7 should be on the top line.
Cards 8, 9 and 10 should be underneath these under 3, 4 and 5.
Cards 11 to 17 should be on the bottom line.

Reading the Cards in a Seventeen Card Spread

For this spread you will be reading the suits of the cards depending on how they fall in the different positions of the spread as given below:

Position One – Personal involvements

Hearts: Activities involving friends and relatives will be successful.

Clubs: An ambitious phase is about to begin. Don't hesitate to seek assistance.

Diamonds: Someone close may try to thwart your efforts to attain your goals.

Spades: Hurdles are ahead but they can be overcome with patience.

Position Two – Fulfilment

Hearts: A special romantic wish could come true.

Clubs: Hard work will bring its just rewards.

Diamonds: A friend interferes with your ambitions.

Spades: Don't be in too much of a rush to achieve your goals.

Position Three- Happiness

Hearts: Anxieties will soon be allayed.

Clubs: Happiness comes through the support of friends and family.

Diamonds: Be grateful for the advice of others but follow your own instincts.

Spades: Optimism helps in the face of difficulties.

Position Four - Future Achievements

Hearts: A special object of desire will soon be within reach.

Clubs: Trust someone who puts an interesting suggestion to you.

Diamonds: Discuss plans with loved ones before putting them into action.

Spades: there may be the need to reconsider certain ambitions.

Position Five – Caution

Hearts: An uncertain situation will call for quick thinking.

Clubs: A recent risk proves to have been worth taking.

Diamonds: Avoid rash decisions concerning money.

Spades: Guard against impetuosity.

Position Six - Secret Wishes
Hearts: Romance is exciting and spontaneous.
Clubs: You can help make a loved one's dream come true.
Diamonds: Ignore others who put doubts into your mind.
Spades: Secret liaisons will not bring happiness.

Position Seven – Social Life
Hearts: You can trust your friends.
Clubs: team efforts bring great rewards.
Diamonds: Friendships are a little strained.
Spade: Be careful who you trust.

Position Eight – Wealth
Hearts: Money is not the problem it used to be.
Clubs: Income will start to increase steadily.
Diamonds: Joint funds need attention.
Spades: Take care in long-term financial deals.

Position Nine – Luck
Hearts: Any changes that occur will be for the best.
Clubs: Luck is linked with friends and associates.
Diamonds: If someone is standing in the way, be sure they don't block your progress.
Spades: Be patient if you don't feel lucky.

Position Ten – Marriage
Hearts: Personal relationships are harmonious.
Clubs: There's a need for some personal freedom.
Diamonds: It's not advisable to rake up past disagreements.
Spades: Tact is needed in loving relationships.

Position Eleven – Inheritance
Hearts: A sizeable legacy is likely but no time is specified.
Clubs: A gift of money is received.
Diamonds: A legal battle concerns money.
Spades: Finances need to be watched. Protect what is rightly yours.

Position Twelve – Rivals
Hearts: Enemies from the past no longer have influence.
Clubs: Friends protect you from a rival.
Diamonds: Differences aren't easily settled.
Spades: An unexpected offer has strings attached.

Position Thirteen – Destiny
Hearts: Strong likelihood of succeeding in chosen profession.
Clubs: Friends help you achieve special targets.
Diamonds: Attaining a long-term goal involves financial risk. Those who dare, win.
Spades: Fate requires you to follow rather than lead.

Position Fourteen – Benefits and Rewards
Hearts: Hard work brings its just rewards.
Clubs: Friends benefit you in some way.
Diamonds: Others may take what should be yours.
Spades: There will be no gain without pain.

Position fifteen – Ambition
Hearts: The future holds much in the way of achievements.
Clubs: Team efforts bring surprising joy.
Diamonds: Keep up with the competition at work.
Spades: Practicality is a must.

Position Sixteen - Rewards
Hearts: Don't be put off when things aren't going your way.
Clubs: Best results come through combined effort.
Diamonds: Someone resents your achievements.
Spades: Use charm when others get in your way.

Position Seventeen - Conclusion
Hearts: Stay steadfast and determined and you'll fulfil your ambitions.
Clubs: Accept help when it is offered. You can't do everything on your own.
Diamonds: Sometimes you have to go it alone to achieve your ambitions.

Spades: Attaining longo-term goals requires dedication, determination and lots of effort.

Layout Example Four:

HORSESHOE SPREAD

Deal out seven cards in the shape of a Horseshoe. From left to right the cards represent:

1 Matters of the past that relate to the present situation
2 The present
3 Developments in the near future
4 Developments that may not be anticipated
5 People in the sitter's life who are linked to the present situation
6 Challenges and difficulties
7 Possible outcomes

Layout Example Five ... Five Card Spreads:

There are a number of ways you can interpret a five-card spread depending on what you are hoping to get out of a reading.

Five card Past and Future Spread:

Deal out five cards from left to right. These cards represent:

1 Past
2 Present
3 Hidden influences
4 New Possibilities
5 Outcome

Five Card Self-Development Spread

Deal out five cards from left to right. These cards represent:

1 How you see yourself
2 How you relate to others
3 What might be causing problems in relationships
4 What can help you improve your relationship with your self and others
5 How you might bring about positive changes in your life

Five Card Situation spread

Deal out five cards from left to right. These cards represent:

1 The situation to be dealt with
2 Your task in order to resolve this situation
3 Issues you are not aware of
4 Possible solution
5 Conclusion/outcome

Examples of readings using some of these spreads can be found in the last chapter.

Layout Example Six:

Pairs

In this spread each position will use two cards that can be read together to represent different areas in life and relationships. From left to right deal two cards, one under the other, five times. You will now have five placements each with two cards.

The first position represents aspects of the sitter.
The next two cards represent the sitter's family and close relationships.
The third placement will have two cards representing the situation as it is now.
Next position shows how the sitter expects the situation to evolve.
The last position will show the likely outcome of the situation.

(iii) The Court Cards

Court cards can represent people (either the sitter or people in their lives) or they can be related to aspects of the sitter's personality.

Both traditional meanings of the cards and modern interpretations will be given. Modern interpretations include a mix of symbolism, intuition and personal insights and experience. You should allow your intuition to guide you to choose the meaning that feels right for the moment.

King of Spades:

Traditional meaning: This spade card could represent a man who is dark haired and ambitious. He may be a work associate who can offer some good career tips or a competitor in business. If he is next to the ace, nine or ten of spades, he may be a widower.

Modern interpretation: The King of Spades can also represent a part of your personality. – A side of you that can achieve good things, once you put your mind to it. In fact you could get results before anyone else has even had a chance to think about it. You will be efficient and sensible about anything you take on. You feel that if a job's worth doing, it's worth doing well and knowing you've carried out something to your best ability is far more satisfying than any praise coming your way. Although of course it's nice to be appreciated once in a while! Past good work is starting to pay off now.

Queen of Spades:

Traditional meaning: This spade card represents a woman with dark hair who could be either a friend with much common sense or a competitor in business. If she is next to the ace, nine or ten of spades, she may be a widow.

Modern interpretation: The Queen of Spades can also represent a part of your personality. – You expect a lot from yourself and others. You have high expectations and you will get annoyed with yourself when you don't meet them. But are you being too rigid in your thinking? You're trying to keep everything structured, controlled and in order. You're trying to be independent and to make firm decisions but it is possible that someone in your life doesn't go along with your way of thinking and this could be a problem. Compromise may be necessary in some areas. Try to put yourself in other people's shoes and this could help you find a middle ground if there are situations of conflict.

Jack of Spades:

Traditional meaning: This card might represent a youth with dark hair. He is likely to be intelligent but sometimes judgemental.

Modern interpretation: There is someone in your life (or your sitter's life) who is quite a character but he also keeps you on your toes. He tends to speak without thinking and this can be amusing at times but sometimes also a little annoying. Or it could be that you have to deal with some pesky correspondence/email matters. – Those little frustrating things that will make you feel better once you get them out of the way. Do these when you think about them as often it's the thought about having to do it that's the worst thing about this situation. Once they're over it will be a relief.

King of Hearts:

Traditional meaning: If the person this reading is for is a fair-haired male, the King of Hearts can be linked to them. If the person this reading is for is female and the Ace of Hearts is near, this card suggests love is strong in her life. Good advice is offered.

Modern interpretation: This card can also suggest aspects of your personality: People will be noticing a new level of maturity about you. You're able to keep your emotions under control and you can sense or at least understand what others are going through. This makes you a great friend to have around when people need advice and help. You'd never turn anyone who is in need, down. You might be planning to take a well-deserved break. – Nothing too long but you have been working hard and it's time you had some fun.

Queen of Hearts:

Traditional meaning: If the person this reading is for is a fair-haired female, the Queen of Hearts can be linked to her. Another suggestion made by this card is that a caring, sensitive and gentle woman in your life is making her presence felt.
Modern interpretation: The Queen of Hearts can represent aspects of your personality: You are a sensitive, kind and loving person. You can be a bit over emotional at times. You prefer to discuss emotions and get it all out rather than keeping it all bottled up inside. You could be a carer a healer or a nurse or you could work with children ... you are good with other people because you have compassion and you care. It may also be that someone needs a shoulder to cry on so watch out for a friend or relative who might need your emotional support.

Jack of Hearts:
Traditional meaning: The Jack of Hearts can represent a fair-haired young man. Pleasant memories are shared.
Modern interpretation: You may have been feeling a little vulnerable or emotional lately. It could be that a relationship that has been meaningful to you is turning out to be more complicated than expected. You have known love that is intense and special but when reality gets in the way it can be more difficult to sustain a close and loving union.

What you are going through now is a big lesson in your emotional development. You could also do with having a little fun. It could be that due to circumstances you have been taking everything so very seriously lately. Now you need to let go a little and try to relax and build up your emotional energy.

King of Clubs:

Traditional meaning: The King of Clubs represents a man with dark hair. He will be good in business and fair in all his dealings. He may be an older male relative, a boss or a senior colleague.
Modern interpretation: If this card refers to an aspect of your personality it is telling you to make good use of your determination to push ahead for what you really want. Channel your energy in positive ways. Focus on your long term goals but don't forget too that you should enjoy fun moments ... life should be a balance of work and play.

Queen of Clubs:

Traditional meaning: The Queen of Clubs can represent a woman with dark hair. She may be a female friend or associate. She will be extravert and confident.
Modern interpretation: If this card refers to an aspect of your personality it suggests you can bring a sense of humour into difficult situations and if things happen to aggravate you, you could never stay annoyed for very long. You give so much support to others but there are times when you too, could do with a little praise and appreciation. If just to keep your spirits up!

Jack of Clubs:

Traditional meaning: The Jack of Clubs can represent a young man with dark hair. If he is a friend, he is someone who can be trusted

Modern interpretation: This card tells you to trust your intuition. Meditate. Push out any doubts, fear and confusion. Get back in touch with your unconscious mind. It may actually be that it will be a sudden and spontaneous move that helps you feel as if you are back on the right track.

King of Diamonds:

Traditional meaning: The King of Diamonds can represent an older man or father figure, a fair-haired man who is likely to be quite powerful.
Modern interpretation: He is someone you have always trusted. Dark hair and dark eyes. He will offer you his support and this will be helpful. At the same time there will be moments when it might feel as if he is making all the decisions or it might feel as if you're on trial. Whatever the situation, he will be a good help to you.
   The path you're on at the moment is a good one for you. This suggests that you should stick with the tried and tested. Don't be tempted to take little detours (or take risks). What seems to be working well for you at the moment is to keep to established routines.

Queen of Diamonds:

Traditional meaning: The Queen of Diamonds might relate to a fair haired woman; a mother figure or a friend who loves to gossip.
Modern interpretation: Current circumstances bring out your motherly instincts. There will be nothing you will like doing better than cooking for others, helping them, guiding them and supporting them. You are an independent person, warm and loving. Or there may be someone close to you who is being supportive: a mentor to you.

Jack of Diamonds:

Traditional meaning: The Jack of Diamonds represents a fair haired youth. This card is associated with renewed hope and anticipation.

Modern interpretation: You have the dreams, the enthusiasm and the desire. You're willing to work hard. All you have to do is find a way to bring your dreams about. Rather than waiting for things to come to you, it might be good to have clear plans for your future. Don't be too vague about it. Start making firm plans and focus on what is realistic and achievable but at the same time, don't be reluctant to look into areas outside your usual field.

Joker: the Joker should be used in card reading. This card can be likened to the court jester or the Fool in the tarot. The Fool can be a naive youngster jumping into new experiences and activities without considering the consequences or the wise man who has been through it all but understands no one will ever know everything. There is always something new to learn. Within the Fool (Joker) lies all the secrets of the universe.

When interpreting the Joker in a reading you might look on the area he represents as an aspect of a person's nature or life that will give some challenge or confrontation. He or she will have to confront this issue and make a decision on it sometime soon. This decision could involve having to weigh up possible risks or whether or not to make some changes, try something new or experiment in different areas of life.

(iv) The Meanings of the Cards

This chapter contains the meanings of the individual playing cards. These are from a mix of traditional meanings and my own interpretations. As you start reading the cards, you too will begin to develop an intuitive understanding of each card and how it relates to life or personality.

The Joker: There is a chance for change and new beginnings. This will help refresh you and make each new day feel like an adventure. You want to live every moment to its fullest. There's a desire to move forward into something new and you should trust the feeling when you get a sense that anything can happen.

The meaning of the Individual Hearts Cards

The Hearts often relate to the water signs Pisces, Cancer and Scorpio. When there are a lot of Hearts in a spread, the sitter is going through an emotional time and their intuition is strong. Love and friendship will also be a strong theme.

Ace of Hearts:
Traditional meaning: Love problems evaporate now. Relationships are more harmonious. Friendliness surrounds you. Good news concerns a relationship. A love letter.
Modern interpretation: This card can suggest the start of new creative or spiritual efforts. It is possible that you feel ready to push out more in these directions. These are areas that will bring you the most contentment at the moment. Putting yourself into projects where you can focus your passion and channel your loving energy will be immensely fulfilling. New relationships or friendships are also possible.

Ten of Hearts:
Traditional meaning: Happiness is likely. You may experience luck and good fortune. This card helps dilute the effect of any unlucky card next to it.
Modern interpretation: Positive things are ahead of you now. You are heading for a time when you will feel more happy and content than you have done in a long while. You might be making a long-term relationship commitment and if so this will be with the right person for you. Or a new relationship will feel like the best thing that has ever happened to you. - Lots of happiness in store and a feeling as if your dreams (probably romantic ones) are being realised.

Nine of Hearts:
Traditional meaning: The wish card. Consider cards next to it. Hearts and diamonds suggest a wish will be fulfilled. Clubs signify the partial fulfilment of a wish. If a spade comes before this card, there may be some disappointment.
Modern interpretation: There's a good blend of emotion, common sense and practicality around you now which is good because in some areas, you feel really happy. It couldn't be better. This may have to do with your relationships, friendships or family life. It might even feel, in some way, as if this is what you have dreamed of all your life. When you look back, this in a sense is the moment you have been waiting for, and yet, strangely, it's not quite how you expected it to be. That's because as we reach one goal and as one wish comes true, there are also lots of other things happening around us. So, we then find we have other goals to aim for and other wishes to make.

Eight of Hearts:
Traditional meaning: Expect an unexpected gift or visitor. Or there may be a party or love invitation winging its way in your direction.

Modern interpretation: You are going through or have just been through a strongly emotional time. There is movement in your cards but this is more related to emotional energy. A situation or relationship which has been important recently is being highlighted by this card. You have invested a lot of emotion in this but you're moving away from it now. It feels strange to you. This is because you've given it so much time and energy that it feels like you're turning your back on it in a way. But a relationship or project isn't quite what you thought it would be. It hasn't brought you the happiness or satisfaction you expected. Or you have achieved the success you desired only suddenly it isn't as important or doesn't mean the same to you anymore. – It's a time of emotional confusion but possible celebratory events in the air, too.

Seven of Hearts:
Traditional meaning: A new friend or associate cannot be trusted. There is some deviousness in relationships. There may be a feeling of loss in love.
Modern interpretation: Confusion is possible. You have a decision to make and this isn't easy. This is because all the possible choices swirling around your head make you more mixed up than you felt before you started thinking. It's hard to know which path to take. Wait for a few days until your thoughts become more focused and your mind grows clearer. Avoid making split second decisions. It's a time when you will discover who your true friends are.

Six of Hearts:
Traditional meaning: A pleasant period is entered. Social affairs are fun. Are you single? You could enjoy a time of partying and getting together with friends.
Modern interpretation: There could be reason to celebrate. At the same time you might find yourself looking back on the past with fond memories. A relationship or friendship brings you happiness and satisfaction.

You might soon be discussing new goals and long-term dreams of a joint nature. Although it can be fun to look back on the past, ahead of you lies your future. Try not to allow past disappointments or frustrations to influence your decisions now.

Five of Hearts:
Traditional meaning: Someone is envious and jealous. This may be you or you could be on the receiving end of another person's envy.
Modern interpretation: Something you longed for or hoped for hasn't turned out the way you expected. You feel as if your hopes have been dashed but don't give up too quickly. Something may have been lost or a relationship may not have gone as you had been expecting, but you could find that there is enough remaining, to build on again. So if you're in a situation where your hopes look completely defeated, don't give up. Instead, try to make use of your high levels of intuition for yourself and not for others. Because deep within your heart you will sense there are other avenues to explore.

Four of Hearts:
Traditional meaning: Travel is a strong possibility. There will be enjoyment through a change of scene. A holiday romance is possible or a romantic holiday with a lover.
Modern interpretation: You're in a good situation at the moment but too good perhaps? It's like everything has settled into a nice routine but you are starting to get little niggles of boredom. You might sense that if you don't find something to get your teeth into soon an aspect of your personality will stagnate. It's good to enjoy a break or a pleasant phase in your life but you should soon be looking for new interests, activities or friendships.
Even if you don't feel you have the energy you will find it. A short holiday might be helpful at this time and it will help you see things from a distant p erspective. – Even just a weekend break. Getting away from your usual surroundings could be helpful.

Three of Hearts:
Traditional meaning: It's difficult to make choices. Other people's opinions are conflicting.
Modern interpretation: The Three of Hearts can bring something special to celebrate. This may be a birthday or anniversary, a special family event or even a marriage. This card highlights a time when you will be having more fun: the chance to party, dance, let your hair down and if no social occasions are planned, to be more creative. It is good to get in touch with your inner child. Don't feel guilty about enjoying yourself and if you can arrange it for just one day even, it might be a great idea to get together with your friends, forget about your troubles and just relax and enjoy their company.

Two of Hearts:
Traditional meaning: A warm, strong partnership is highlighted by this card. An engagement or a wedding is possible. Partnerships are harmonious.
Modern interpretation: You could be at the beginning stage of a new arrangement, friendship or partnership. There's a lot of love around you and something special about a relationship. This is a delightfully loving phase of your life if you are already in an established partnership. Generally a feeling that any joint dealings you are entering into now should be harmonious.

(iv) The Meaning of the Individual Cards

Clubs Cards

A predominance of Clubs in a spread suggest: ambition, striving towards goals and the sitter's social and professional reputation.

Ace of Clubs:
Traditional meaning: A job offer is likely or the start of a venture that needs skill and effort in order to be successful. Health is good. Papers, letters or contracts will involve money.
Modern interpretation: Good working relationships or the possibility of a new boss or new systems being introduced into the workplace. The Ace of Clubs suggests new career opportunities or exciting new directions in relation to your own ambitions. This is the card that helps keep you feeling positive and it shows, too, all the energy you have that will help you fulfil your ambitions. For new ideas will be so exciting that you will feel a gush of energy that you will want to put towards them. You feel inspired and can't wait to get new plans underway. You might feel drawn to a fascinating new interest or hobby ... new starts are likely that will require creative, fiery energy.

Ten of Clubs:
Traditional meaning: Prosperity. Wealth. A journey.
Modern interpretation: A job offer is likely if you are looking for work. Success in business can be expected now. You may undertake a long distance journey or will be in contact with people from abroad. Appointments and meetings will be official in nature. You might be attending an interview, taking exams or waiting to hear the outcome of recent tests or meetings. In which case unless other cards in the spread suggest differently, the results should be to your liking.

Nine of Clubs:
Traditional meaning: You will see the completion of past hard work. A special goal is reached. Possibly an inheritance.
Modern interpretation: You have been through a lot lately and some of this may have been painful. It will take time for you to heal from these emotional wounds. This too is keeping you standing still. You're doing your best to keep other people smiling. You're getting on as best as you can although there have been moments when you just wanted to curl up and hide from it all. Yet you are finding the strength within you to get up and face another day. You should be proud of yourself for how you are handling your present situation and how you have handled past difficulties. You are about to enter a phase where you can recoup your energy and heal. So, you have been working really hard and there will be some form of success or recognition. Out of this situation you will feel stronger and more determined.

Eight of Clubs:
Traditional meaning: Responsibilities increase. New duties are taken on. There may be some opposition in business.
Modern interpretation: Focused activity and movement is likely now. You have lots of raw energy and passion to put into your goals. Provided you are certain about where you are heading and all distractions have been removed, you should be able to devote yourself to the task in hand with absolute concentration and determination. You will keep at it until it is complete. You will be making positive accomplishments, feeling productive and you will also be proud of what you're able to get done in a short space of time.

Seven of Clubs:
Traditional meaning: Success is likely in business after a lot of effort. A promotion is possible or a job move that is beneficial but be patient.

Modern interpretation: Life can be quite a struggle and you've overcome a lot of obstacles to get where you are now but you're almost in the frame of mind that you're wondering whether it's time to give up. Will it be worth it? Are you fighting a losing battle?

Will you ever see the light at the end of the tunnel? Don't give up yet! Keep going for a short while longer and you will feel it was all definitely worth it. So keep at it. This isn't the time to admit defeat.

Six of Clubs:

Traditional meaning: Funding, loans or financial help will be received. It's a good time to make financial applications.

Modern interpretation: There's a strong sense of achievement. After all the struggles you've been through, at last the moment has arrived when you feel it has all been worth it. You made the right decisions. You took the right action and this is clear to you now. Better still, you are about to reap the rewards for all your hard work. It could be that you will be offered a contract, a commission or a well-deserved promotion ... generally you will feel you are moving forward thanks to efforts of the past.

Five of Clubs:

Traditional meaning: There's a competitive feel to relationships. Social life will have its ups and downs.

Modern interpretation: There's a strange feel to a relationship that is important to you or this could be within a group of people. It's like there's a competitive atmosphere but friendly too. Someone might like to tease and throw challenges to others but not in a negative way. It's more to keep everything interesting and so life doesn't get too boring.

In some areas of your life you might feel you aren't able to move forward because of what is going on around you. Instead of being able to work together with some people and reach agreements, it's as if someone is constantly disagreeing with what you say or asking you to explain yourself.

When you can't get on the same wave-length it's unlikely you will make any progress. It could be that if you all sit down calmly together and discuss your feelings you may be able to resolve the situation in a way that makes you feel you can start to move forward with more confidence.

Four of Clubs:
Traditional meaning: Be careful about who you trust. Someone is being devious.
Modern interpretation: Take a break. Enjoy a breather. Stop and smell the flowers.
You really deserve to treat yourself because you have been working hard. It's time to have a little fun. At the same time you can't take your eye off your goals. So you might enjoy a little pampering ... like having a weekend away but it's back to work on Monday ... there is that kind of feel to this card. So things are going quite well and you should be pleased with your progress.

Three of Clubs:
Traditional meaning: New long-term commitments in close relationships are agreed on. Marriage is a possibility. Money will be received.
Modern interpretation: Most things are going well for you at the moment. You should be feeling confident and pleased with yourself and that's because past efforts are starting to bring rewards your way. You have been working hard towards something and other people are showing you more respect because they can see you are taking your responsibilities seriously. Don't feel you aren't good enough if you're mixing with older or more experienced people. You have a lot to bring into conversations and group activities and others too could benefit from your ideas.

Two of Clubs:
Traditional meaning: Some hurdles ahead in relationships and business. Gossip could cause problems. A warning not to listen to rumours.

Modern interpretation: You have more control than you think. You would have preferred to have had more time to come to terms with some issues. That's why it's feeling so strange and unnerving. You haven't felt as if you've been able to prepare. There are some obstacles before you but if you stay strong and take action you will be able to overcome these. An opportunity you are presented with could come as a huge surprise. There will be some excitement as well as nerves associated with this.

The clubs in an ordinary playing card deck are associated with the Wands in the tarot. These cards represent the fire signs: Aries, Leo and Sagittarius. They are associated with action, business, work, health and energy.

The Meaning of the Individual Spades Cards

Spades are the most serious cards in the deck, representing areas in which the sitter must be cautious and careful. When there are more spade cards than any other, it could be there is some contention in their life or someone is trying to evade responsibilities.

Spades are sometimes associated with the winter, when considering the timing of the cards. They are linked with the air signs Gemini, Libra and Aquarius and when representing a person in the sitter's life, this person is likely to be intelligent and logical.

Meaning of the Spade Cards

These are the basic interpretations of spade cards when they appear in a spread. When you do a reading, they should be weighed up with the other cards alongside them.

Ace of Spades:
Traditional meaning: Visiting a tall spacious building. An intense conflict.
Modern interpretation: The Ace of Spades can represent a flash of insight or mental clarity. That 'aha' moment when everything suddenly starts to make sense in your mind. This can bring about a new understanding of matters which have caused problems in the past. With the fog now cleared from your mind this would be a good time for ending old commitments and making new starts that involve mental work. This can be anything from writing a book, setting up a website, starting a blog, joining or setting up a reading group or writers' circle.
This card can signify some form of disappointment or a situation that is likely to come to an end and this will cause emotional stress. Always remember however that as one chapter closes, another one will begin.

Ten of Spades:
Traditional meaning: This card is indication of some sadness and worry. Someone may be recuperating from an accident. If you had a wish on your mind when the cards were being dealt, it could be that what you long for won't yet be happening.

Modern interpretation: The Ten of Spades suggests there are aspects of your life that are weighing heavily on you now. You know what it feels like to have a lot of challenge and to have been through hardship; also to wonder if ever things will get any better. Sometimes you might feel as if someone else has all the control and you're powerless to do anything about it but this isn't true. When things take a turn for the worse, you might have a tendency to push your own needs aside. You would rather see other people happy even if this means you have to make all the sacrifices. But the time will soon be here for you to make some changes. You know this deep in your heart and you are ready because there are some burdens that have got heavier and now the load is too much. You need to find a way to break free.

Nine of Spades:
Traditional meaning: You could be feeling emotionally low. Irritability could lead to quarrels. Too much responsibility might have a negative effect on health.

Modern interpretation: Something is or has been causing you a lot of worry. This may be about someone's health or a stressful situation. There is a lot of anxiety and maybe you've been having trouble sleeping? It's easier said than done but try to tell yourself that worry solves nothing and can be a waste of energy. When you do sleep, you might wake up feeling you have had bad dreams or feeling as tired as you did when you went to bed. It can be hard to find a sense of direction when you're feeling low or anxious or even a little lonely.

Some relationships in your life could be better. Have you experienced another person's cruelty: emotional or psychological? Whatever the situation, there is something causing you worry and you feel ready to find a way to lift yourself out of this. Don't doubt yourself any more.

Eight of Spades:
Traditional meaning: You might be thinking about new options but you should be wary of new paths as they could lead to misfortune.
Modern interpretation: A situation or relationship has been causing you a lot of worry. It has probably kept you awake at night, tossing and turning and wondering whether things would get any better. Anxiety could make it seem a lot worse in your mind. Try to calm your thoughts as what you are worried about could turn out to be nowhere as near as bad as you are expecting. It would be better too to face your problems rather than keep worrying about them. After all, worrying will not solve anything.

Seven of Spades:
Traditional meaning: Someone will offer advice that could be misleading. A friend is not all he or she appears. You should be careful about who they trust.
Modern interpretation: There's a feeling as if someone's not being entirely honest with you ... someone in your life that you don't trust. Or could it be that you are holding information back because you know if someone finds out about it they will use it to their own advantage? It may be that you will have to be a little sneaky in some areas in order to get what you want or to find out information that someone else is reluctant to share with you. There may be some form of loss.

Six of Spades:
Traditional meaning: This card warns of possible mistakes. It will be important to think before taking action. The good news is: some areas of their life will start to show improvement.

Modern interpretation: If it feels like you've hit a rocky patch in a relationship or work situation or indeed any situation in your life, things should slowly start to improve. They will get better and easier. You will eventually start to move forwards. It's like you will be leaving the storm behind you and moving into calmer waters. There may be a journey ahead or you might be planning a holiday. Even just a few days break might sound like a good idea at the moment. It may also be that a friend is moving on or moving into a new home or someone you work with is changing jobs.

Five of Spades:
Traditional meaning: Some form of disappointment is likely and this could relate to a close relationship. This card speaks of loss. You should not listen to gossip and should make your own decisions.
Modern interpretation: Little things might keep going wrong or plans don't turn out as you hoped. For instance, something you apply for may not be quite what you expected, plans may be delayed or deadlines could be missed through no fault of your own. It's frustrating when things go wrong but if you're giving it your best shot, there is little else you can do.

Four of Spades:
Traditional meaning: You will soon have to make some difficult business decisions. Someone else wants what you have. This is a very stressful period.
Modern interpretation: Generally you're reaching a stage where you need to take a break, just to give your body a chance to relax and your mind a chance to unwind. Take a trip to a favourite place that's soothing for your body and soul. This would be a good time to think about your life, review where you are and work out where you want to go. Sometimes standing back from the situation helps you see it more clearly.

Three of Spades:
Traditional meaning: An ending is likely. This could relate to a romantic or business relationship. Sometimes this card indicates a third person is breaking into a relationship.

Modern interpretation: A situation you are going through will have a powerful effect on your emotions. It's good to be able to say that you can put the past behind you now and you are moving on to the path of recovery. You will discover there are things in life that can make you very happy. So it can be very hard to move on from this type of situation but you will be doing your best to leave it all behind. Don't get annoyed with yourself if at times you still feel the pain and upset; give yourself a chance to grieve and as the tears dry, new doors of experience will open up to you.

Two of Spades:
Traditional meaning: Gossip is not to be trusted. A disagreement could be the result of listening to the wrong people. Deceit is in the air.
Modern interpretation: Who do you trust? People might say they mean well when they offer you advice but do they have an ulterior motive? It might even seem as if your mind is playing cruel tricks on you, making you doubt yourself. To make good decisions you need to start trusting your intuition. Let go of fears. Push your worries aside and ignore self-doubt. Your problem could be that you are spending so much time worrying that you're going to make the wrong decision that you are holding yourself back from taking advantage of new opportunities.

Although spades aren't negative cards, they do point to areas of responsibility or where watchfulness is recommended.

The Meaning of the Individual Diamond Cards

A predominance of Diamonds in a spread highlights money and communications. They might point to a logical, practical person who is a good communicator

Ace of Diamonds:
Traditional meaning: An important message is received. This can be good news or disappointing depending on whether this card is upright or reversed and dependent too, on other cards in the spread.
Modern interpretation: You're focused now on the realisation of your goals and very soon you will see them taking shape as you had hoped. You will start noticing results for your efforts. Alongside commitments you already have, something new is beginning. Your cash situation will be improving. There's a chance of new beginnings and this might affect your finances. It is possible that some money is on its way but if so, you already know what you're going to spend it on.

Ten of Diamonds:
Traditional meaning: Happiness might be found in travel. Communications from a distant place will be lucky. Changes that occur now will be fortunate.
Modern interpretation: Generally there is a positive feel around you but it isn't a time to take risks or gamble with your money. There's some restlessness ... wanting something different maybe to shake your life up a little. Life can be very peaceful for you now but you might look back on a time when you were more active and when you enjoyed a challenge. You're starting to wonder whether it might be a good idea to find something new to get your teeth into.

Nine of Diamonds:
Traditional meaning: The Nine of Diamonds is linked with new career opportunities. A possible money surprise. – Working as a team might bring what cannot be achieved alone.

Modern interpretation: New doors of opportunity are about to open for you. This will relate to your career or financial matters. The receipt of a bonus or unexpected sum of money could make a pleasing difference to your finances. It's a great time to redecorate or make improvements to your home, purchase items for your house or garden.

Eight of Diamonds:
Traditional meaning: Money situation could be changing, whether for the better or worse will depend on whether this card is upright or reversed and other cards in the spread. Marriage is a possibility or setting up a joint financial arrangement.
Modern interpretation: You're starting to understand that you must put in the effort to achieve your goals or for financial reward. It might be a good time to think about doing a training course or signing up on a workshop. – Or doing some kind of practical training that might help enhance your earning potential in the future. This could even be developing existing skills or learning new ones that might be useful in the long-term. Also, this card suggests that a great way to get rid of any nervous energy will be through doing some practical work around the house or garden. It's a great phase in your life for getting things done.

Seven of Diamonds:
Traditional meaning: All pros and cons should be weighed up before serious decisions are made. News received will come as some surprise.
Modern interpretation: Keep telling yourself that you are making progress even if sometimes it seems a little tedious and it takes time for things to grow. All good things come to those who wait.
   It's also like there is plenty for you to do. A lot of hard work but do you feel your efforts aren't being appreciated? This seems to be a tiring time for you. It may also be that you're doing voluntary work or helping other people so you are giving so much to others but what about you?

New seeds are being sewn in your life now and they will start to grow. You will start to expand and grow. There may be no sign yet of this but the way you are feeling: your confusion and restlessness is already a sign that you are heading for something new.

Six of Diamonds:
Traditional meaning: To achieve goals, effort must be made. Gossip or interference from other people could cause problems in a close relationship.
Modern interpretation: Sometimes, in certain areas, it's important to be broad. You can spread your energy over a wide range of activities and succeed in getting results too. Other times it's important to be precise. So it's worth thinking about setting yourself small achievable goals over the weeks ahead. If for instance you're thinking about getting healthy, you might decide to walk 2,000 steps a day for a week. Or to eat fresh vegetables and healthy food instead of grabbing a quick unhealthy snack when you get the time. If you're striving towards something important, keep records. List your goals and then move your goal posts higher as you start to reach them. ... The main thing to aim for is progress, not perfection.

Five of Diamonds:
Traditional meaning: Friends and colleagues will be supportive. A letter, text message or email will contain good news or bad depending on the other cards in the spread.
Modern interpretation: You are going through a difficult phase. When you're struggling financially and there are other tense things going on in your life you can't help but lose a little faith in yourself too. It's as if your optimism is being worn down daily and you're struggling to find the energy to move forward. There is no easy solution but it is possible to rebuild your finances, restore your faith in yourself and find your positivity again.

Because this card also suggests the situation is changing and you will feel as if the struggles you are going through will be worth it in some way when you look back on this. Because it may not be apparent how at the moment, but this could lead to something of lasting value.

Four of Diamonds:
Traditional meaning: Decisions will have something to do with home and family life and expenses related to this. There may be an improvement in money coming into the home. Someone might receive an inheritance.
Modern interpretation: You are in a more stable position than you have been for a while. Yet because you know what it is to suffer and you have been through hardship, you are being really careful about the way you handle finances. You would never take unnecessary risks, for instance. You are protective of what you have built up so far because it has taken a lot of hard work to get to this position.

You are a self-sufficient person both emotionally and financially. You can be independent and at the moment may even prefer it to be this way. It's as if you've been through so much and put in so much effort to get this far you don't want to do anything to jeopardise all you have worked for. But is this making you maybe a little too cautious or too afraid to make any changes for fear of losing all you now have?

Also, there's a little niggle growing within you that maybe you can do better. – That maybe it's time to look at new choices for the future.

Three of Diamonds:
Traditional meaning: Correspondence may be linked to financial or legal matters.
Modern interpretation: You are starting to plan for the future and lay down the foundations for something new in your life to begin. This could be centred on your job, like taking some form of further training in order to improve your current situation.

Or if it is a relationship, your idea is to work on ways to improve your current conditions. You want to adapt to a situation and make improvements so it can be even better. There may be some paperwork to sign or agreements reached and again you may be looking at your financial situation and thinking of ways to improve it or save for the future. – Maybe for something specific like a new car, computer or holiday. Although a lot of focus is on practical matters, it's a positive focus and in many ways you feel hopeful.

Two of Diamonds:
Traditional meaning: Joint matters may attract hostility from others. There is a need for caution in romance.
Modern interpretation: If a business partnership is being discussed, be sure all agreements are written down in black and white.
  Eventually you will need to get a better balance between work and play. You need to have some fun too and you shouldn't feel guilty about pampering yourself occasionally. Currently you have the energy to keep going and you will enjoy a challenge. Good things are happening. You feel you are making progress and learning about yourself at the same time. If new opportunities arise and these appeal to you, this card suggests you should go for it.

Energy and enthusiasm can be high when many diamonds appear in a spread. Goals can be achieved with a positive attitude. Diamonds are the first suit in the deck and can also be related to the time of the year associated with the sign Aries.

(v) How to weave the cards in a Spread Together

As you read the spread, if anything comes to you intuitively, trust your feelings. Remember that the meanings of the cards given in this book should only be used as a basis on which to begin your readings. Eventually you will start to notice certain events happen whenever a particular card comes up and you will begin to link your own meanings to each card, either in addition to or instead of the interpretations in this book.

As you read the cards, linking them to whichever position they fall in the spread, you will also find yourself weaving the meanings of the cards together. – Some will support the others. Some will seem to cancel out each other's meanings in which case you balance all you see until you feel it makes sense to you.

Traditionally there are meanings for set combinations. This book does not always rely on the traditional meanings of the cards but more on interpretations the author has found works for her. Even so, in order to give an example of how the meanings of cards can be combined if they fall near each other in a spread, the following suggestions are a mix of traditional meanings and the author's own interpretations. – Again, when reading combinations, your intuition is always the best guide.

Meanings of Combinations Involving Aces:

Two Aces (red): A relationship commitment or new joint financial agreements
Two Aces (black): Beginning of a training course/academic degree or advanced study course
Three Aces: New starts in a few areas of life which will have a major effect on general circumstances
Four Aces: Big changes ahead. New directions. Possibly a move.

Ace of Clubs with Jack of Clubs: Good news concerning relationship matters or a job; a proposal or proposition

Ace of Clubs with Ten of Clubs: Passionate encounters; exciting new arrangements in existing relationships; family celebrations

Ace of Diamonds with Four of Clubs: Financial or career transactions initiated now will lead to a stable and secure future

Ace of Diamonds with Ten of Clubs: A marriage or long-term commitment that will be profitable emotionally and financially

Ace of Diamonds with Eight of Clubs: A profitable new business arrangement or a job offer with an increase in income

Ace of Diamonds with Ten of Spades: What appears to be an exciting new possibility could have strings attached; new arrangements could bring huge responsibility

Ace of Diamonds with Ten of Diamonds: Anything initiated now regarding money or career should have a successful outcome

Ace of Clubs with Three of Diamonds: New business deals should be successful and profitable

Ace of Clubs with Ten of Diamonds: Career and money affairs should start to improve

Ace of Clubs with Four of Clubs: Learning new skills or taking on new career assignments will bring future security

Ace of Spades with Ten of Diamonds: Although the responsibility will be heavy, new commitments will bring material rewards

Ace of Spades with Three of Clubs: The possibility of new friendships or romance being formed in the workplace

As with the Aces and examples above, all the cards can be woven together to enhance their individual meanings.

Significance of Numbers in a Reading

When reading a spread, look at how the meaning of one card might balance another. Do two cards support each other to reinforce any impressions you might get? As well as reading the individual cards and how they relate to each other, there are other factors you might look at to give depth to your reading. Look at the numbers on the cards. Are there two or more of a single number? Look at the balance of suits in a reading. Does one suit stand out to have more influence than the others?

What does it mean when two or more of a single number shows in a spread? Here are some suggestions:

Two or more Aces show a surge of energy which can either be focused on achieving a specific aim or will die out quickly if not channelled properly.

Two or more Twos show a strong chance of partnerships being formed or ended. Joint arrangements being made or two people going their separate ways. A choice of where to direct energy so as not to channel it in the wrong direction.

Two or more Threes show an idea, project or situation has reached a comfortable stage. Progress is being made but there is still more to do. The foundations have been laid and can be built upon.

Two or more Fours show there is opportunity to build solid foundations for the future either through putting time and effort into a meaningful relationship or a project that can bring more security into the sitter's life.

Two or more Fives show a need to guard against loss. Some areas of life will be out of kilter. Problems and difficulties to overcome.

Two or more Sixes show that balance from recent disharmonies will be restored. There will be inner harmony after emotional turmoil.

Two or more Sevens show challenges that need to be faced. There's a need to look for a way to overcome problems. This may involve standing firm where there is conflict or opposition.

Two or more Eights shows the sitter will have the skills and experience to draw on in order to progress.

Two or more Nines show a goal or special stage in life has been reached but a gap in life remains and discovering this missing element will bring ultimate satisfaction.

Two or more Tens show a circle is complete. A chapter in life is ending. – Completion and a sense of fulfilment. Possibility of travel.

Reading with Colours and Numbers

This chapter is devoted to a spread that will only use numbers and colours for your interpretations of the cards. So for this one, you will only be using the numbered cards of each suit. Separate these from the rest of the deck and shuffle.

Deal out Seven cards face down in the shape of a horseshoe. Deal out another seven cards face down directly on top of the ones you have just dealt out.

When reading these cards, the positions in this spread will represent:

Position One: Past events that affect the present situation.
Position Two: Challenges and difficulties to overcome.
Position three: Present situation.
Position Four: Choices ahead.
Position Five: Factors that need to be taken into consideration.
Position Six: Possible outcome of one decision.
Position Seven: Possible outcome of second choice.

To read these cards you will firstly be concentrating on the numbers. Go to position one and reveal the two cards. Add up the numbers of these cards and write it down. i.e. two of clubs and seven of diamonds would equal nine.

Now with the remaining six positions do the same. Add up the number of the cards in each of the positions and write them down.

Remembering to incorporate the meaning of the placement in this reading, look up the numbers you have on your sheet in the interpretations below. This will give a general meaning of the number. See if you can tune into your intuition and get more.

Meaning of the numbers of the cards:

CARDS ADD UP TO TWO:
When related to situation/circumstances: You are likely to find yourself moving about in more than one direction. This can make it difficult for you to stay focused on any one goal.
When related to challenges to overcome: There will be increased pressure for you to succeed but what other people expect from you may not be what you want for yourself.
When related to choices/decisions: Communicate your ideas with those who may be able to help you.
When related to outcomes: You can use charm and encouragement to sweet talk others into cooperating with you rather than competing against you.

CARDS ADD UP TO THREE:
When related to situation/circumstances: Your creativity flows, you have the passion and enthusiasm that will attract positive opportunities your way.
When related to challenges to overcome: Persevere and you will take several steps forward towards the achievement of a personal dream.
When related to choices/decisions: Your intuition is reliable. Trust your instincts.
When related to outcomes: Romance could be blossoming in your life soon. New developments may bring a rise in income or confidence.

CARDS ADD UP TO FOUR:

When related to situation/circumstances: You will soon have something to celebrate with your family.

When related to challenges to overcome: Your home and family life could be affected by business tensions and outside pressures.

When related to choices/decisions: Seeds are beginning to take root. Now is not the time to change direction.

When related to outcomes: Conscientious and careful efforts will be planting the seeds for your future security.

CARDS ADD UP TO FIVE:

When related to situation/circumstances: The further you cast your net, the better your chances of success.

When related to challenges to overcome: The urge to do something different and new is making itself felt very strongly.

When related to choices/decisions: Consider a broader range of activities and life will be more fulfilling.

When related to outcomes: Your creative and imaginative instincts will soon reach new heights.

CARDS ADD UP TO SIX:

When related to situation/circumstances: A lot of your focus and attention will be riveted on career responsibilities, a work situation or a health matter.

When related to challenges to overcome: New routines could well enable you to operate more efficiently and effectively.

When related to choices/decisions: Decisions you now make could make an important difference to your career or job situation and long-term hopes.

When related to outcomes: Build on new opportunities and your position will be stronger.

CARDS ADD UP TO SEVEN:
When related to situation/circumstances: Combining forces with a partner could help give you the confidence to keep at it and succeed.
When related to challenges to overcome: A challenge will bring out the best in you and could be both exciting and nerve-wracking at the same time.
When related to choices/decisions: Find ways to right whatever wrongs have befallen you and this will open doors to help you move forward in a more positive direction.
When related to outcomes: An unexpected problem may arise but you will be determined not to let this beat you and you will quickly pick up the pieces and look for another way to resolve the situation.

CARDS ADD UP TO EIGHT:
When related to situation/circumstances: You should take up an opportunity to gain the knowledge or skills that are lacking. This can relate to a job situation or self-development.
When related to challenges to overcome: Choose wisely and you will make headway in a personal ambition.
When related to choices/decisions: A promotion, certificate or award will be offered as reward for your past hard work or enterprising suggestions.
When related to outcomes: Make the most of opportunities to better yourself or make a name for yourself.

CARDS ADD UP TO NINE:
When related to situation/circumstances: Get prepared for some big happiness.
When related to challenges to overcome: Look for the best opportunities to expand your emotional happiness and improve your family life.
When related to choices/decisions: There may be enjoyment in new or unfamiliar surroundings as a result of a spontaneous decision.
When related to outcomes: Soon you will be experiencing more freedom and less restriction.

CARDS ADD UP TO TEN:
When related to situation/circumstances: You are in a stronger position than you realise now. You should have more confidence in yourself and faith in your abilities.
When related to challenges to overcome: Opportunities will seem to appear out of thin air a times. Don't hesitate to act.
When related to choices/decisions: The right decision will help you take steps towards a special and meaningful goal.
When related to outcomes: Circumstances that your present situation is leading to will make you feel more content and secure.

CARDS ADD UP TO ELEVEN:
When related to situation/circumstances:
Relationships thrive where there is respect. Without trust and respect a friendship or romance will have no substance.
When related to challenges to overcome: You may actually enjoy trying to solve problems and difficulties that give you a chance to stretch your mind and imagination.
When related to choices/decisions: It's make your mind up time. You need to choose between one of two directions.
When related to outcomes: Be ready to re-structure existing commitments before inviting anything new into your life.

CARDS ADD UP TO TWELVE:
When related to situation/circumstances: Relationships are moving forward. Partners and loved ones are more generous about sharing their feelings and other gifts.
When related to challenges to overcome: Difficulties that face you could well sort themselves out in their own time if you leave them be.
When related to choices/decisions: A personal decision or choice to do with your private life should not be delayed any longer. Hesitation could lead to lost opportunity.

When related to outcomes: The more practical you are in your planning, the more realistic in your expectations, the more chance you have of succeeding.

CARDS ADD UP TO THIRTEEN:
When related to situation/circumstances: You are gaining control of your situation and will feel more settled, emotionally and financially.

When related to challenges to overcome: Rather than be defensive, try not to let challenges upset you. Relax and it will appear to others that you are in control even if you feel far from it.

When related to choices/decisions: New ideas or choices will have results that are beyond the scope of your current vision.

When related to outcomes: An enforced or unexpected delay or postponement could turn out to be to your long-term benefit.

CARDS ADD UP TO FOURTEEN:
When related to situation/circumstances: Find the courage you need to take the steps necessary to improve your circumstances.

When related to challenges to overcome: Whatever challenges might face you, you will be determined to deal with them. Find the most sensible option to deal with the situation.

When related to choices/decisions: Your hope is that your decisions will enable you to enjoy events that are to come and this will give you a lot of anticipatory pleasure.

When related to outcomes: Keep emotions flowing freely. This helps you tune into your intuition which in turn will lead you in the right direction.

CARDS ADD UP TO FIFTEEN:
When related to situation/circumstances: You are making good progress now so curb any desire to take short-cuts.

When related to challenges to overcome: Your determination is admired by others. Persistence will take you far.

When related to choices/decisions: A number of what-ifs make it hard for you to make a firm choice. You're allowing trivial matters to prey on your mind.

When related to outcomes: Dust off those childhood dreams. You're about to discover it is never too late to realise your true potential.

CARDS ADD UP TO SIXTEEN:

When related to situation/circumstances: Once a spark has been lit it can flare up very quickly and a situation might seem to grow out of control.

When related to challenges to overcome: A trace of uncertainty or worry is creeping into your thoughts but you could find you have no need to be anxious.

When related to choices/decisions: Refuse to let feelings of frustration, anger and annoyance get mixed up so you take your feelings out on the wrong person.

When related to outcomes: You're ready for something new and refreshing.

CARDS ADD UP TO SEVENTEEN:

When related to situation/circumstances: A creative exercise or project will be fun and refreshing.

When related to challenges to overcome: You will find a way to break out of a restricting situation.

When related to choices/decisions: Think about how you might use your skills and knowledge in new ways in the future.

When related to outcomes: You will be able to turn circumstances to your advantage.

CARDS ADD UP TO EIGHTEEN:

When related to situation/circumstances: You have a good idea about what the weeks ahead are likely to hold. You can trust your intuition.

When related to challenges to overcome: A sense of purpose is with you now and this will help you deal effectively with any problems.

When related to choices/decisions: Choices could lead you to exciting new areas.

When related to outcomes: New developments in your life will bring you great pleasure and joy.

CARDS ADD UP TO NINETEEN:

When related to situation/circumstances: You feel moved to break free from a situation or circumstances that have become overly familiar. A change of routine might do you the world of good.

When related to challenges to overcome: Try to embrace the changes that are about to happen as they could be changes for the better.

When related to choices/decisions: Make good use of your imagination when deciding on what you want to do.

When related to outcomes: Exciting events are ahead.

CARDS ADD UP TO TWENTY:

When related to situation/circumstances: You need to feel you are going in the right direction and this may mean taking a new look at your situation.

When related to challenges to overcome: You feel under pressure to do well in a joint or group situation. There's a sense that if you fail you are letting other people down.

When related to choices/decisions: Someone close could make some intriguing and interesting suggestions.

When related to outcomes: New knowledge will be gained through listening to others.

Finally to complete the reading, is there a predominance of red or black in the fourteen cards in this spread?

If red is strong: emotions and spiritual impressions are vivid and feelings are strong. The sitter will be experiencing some emotional situations. There will be some focus on material matters and ways to establish a sense of security.

If black is strong: communications, paperwork and business concerns are being highlighted. The sitter will be dealing with several challenges and looking for ways to resolve problems.

(vii) Quick Ways to Answer a Question

There will times when you might want to use your cards to quickly answer a question that's on your mind or to help you make a decision. Here are two methods you can use to do this.

Aces and Answering Questions

Shuffle your cards and as you shuffle them keep the question you want answered in your mind. When you are ready, deal thirteen cards out in a fan on the table. Now scan these cards. Are there any Aces? If so put them to one side. Return the remaining cards back to the pack. All the cards (minus the Aces you have put aside) should be shuffled again with your question on your mind. Again deal out thirteen cards as before. Check again for Aces and put these to one side. Repeat this once more. As you put the Aces to one side, keep them in the order they have shown up.

   The earlier the Aces appear, the more positive an outcome is likely. So if an Ace or more Aces appear in the first deal this is particularly fortunate. If in the second, it is still a good sign. If in the third the consequences will be reasonable but not as good as expected. If no Aces turn up during the three deals you might expect the outcome to be a negative one.

   Now consider the order in which they have shown up. If a Heart shows first and the question was about a relationship, the answer is the one you are hoping for. Go with it. This is a good sign for relationship and creative ventures. If a Spade shows first you might expect obstacles and difficulties ahead. If a Diamond shows first, there may be material benefits out of the situation. The outcome will generally be good. If a Club shows first, the results will be positive but effort will be involved.

Answering a Yes/No Question

A quick way to answer a yes/no question is to shuffle the cards with your question on your mind. Now draw three cards. If there are two reds and one black, the answer is yes. If there are two blacks and one red: the answer is no. Three reds means yes, three blacks: no.

(viii) Personality and Destiny Card

Through a combination of astrology, numbers and symbolism, each of the numbered cards in every suit can be linked with a birth date to give a summary of a person's life and character. Look up your birthdate to find your personality and destiny card.

1st to 10th January – Five of Spades
11th to 20th January – Six of spades
21st to 30th January – Seven of Spades
1st to 10th February - Eight of Spades
11th to 20th February – Nine of Spades
21st to 30th February – Ten of spades
1st to 10th March – Two of Diamonds
11th to 20th March – Three of Diamonds
21st to 30th March – Four of Diamonds
1st to 10th April – Five of Diamonds
11th to 20th April – Six of Diamonds
21st to 30th April - Seven of Diamonds
1st to 10th May – Eight of Diamonds
11th to 20th May – Nine of Diamonds
21st to 30th May – Ten of Diamonds
1st to 10th June – Two of Hearts
11th to 20th June – Three of Hearts
21st to 30th June – Four of Hearts
1st to 10th July – Five of Hearts
11th to 20th July – Six of Hearts
21st to 30th July – Seven of Hearts
1st to 10th August – Eight of Hearts
11th to 20th August – Nine of Hearts
21st to 30th August – Ten of Hearts
1st to 10th September – Two of Clubs
11th to 20th September – Three of Clubs
21st to 30th September Four of Clubs
1st to 10th October – Five of Clubs
11th to 20th October – Six of Clubs
21st to 30th October – Seven of Clubs
1st to 10th November – Eight of Clubs

11th to 20th November – Nine of Clubs
21st to 30th November - Ten of Clubs
1st to 10th December – Two of Spades
11th to 20th December – Three of Spades
21st to 30th December – Four of Spades

What does your Personality and Destiny card say about you?

Look up your card below to read what it says about your personality. When your Personality and Destiny Card comes up in a reading, this signifies that any changes that are occurring now will be for a reason: they are meant to be. This card, in a spread, will also add power to decisions you are now making.

Five of Spades: You have a strong drive towards security and will work hard towards attaining this. It may be through material values such as work, money and ambition or through establishing happy relationships in your home and family life but your main focus is on making your life as secure as possible. You have a strong sense of responsibility and a lot of determination and endurance. You have great inner reserves and people find you cool in a crisis.
Six of Spades: You strive to be successful in all that you do. You try to do this within the rules of society. You respect tradition and get frustrated with people who rebel for the sake of being rebellious. You have a strong practical side and can be determined in the face of obstacles. You have good business sense and will work hard in order to move up a notch or two on the success ladder.

Seven of Spades: Yours is a complex personality that few people if any are able to say they truly understand. You have a love of freedom, both for yourself and for others. Friends will say you can be unpredictable and no-one will know what you're going to do next. You are generous towards those who are less fortunate than yourself. There is a strong humanitarian side to your nature that leads you to doing regular volunteer work throughout your life.

Eight of Spades: On the face of it you might be a bit of a rebel but you aren't a rebel without a cause. You do not rebel just for the sake of it. To some you might appear wayward or a bit unruly but you will not follow rules that have no reason. You will not respect authority when that respect hasn't been earned. Anyone who presents you with rigid and confining rules also presents you with a challenge as you will find ways of getting round rules and regulations that appear to have no purpose.

Nine of Spades: You love your personal freedom and have a strong independent side to your nature. Friends and acquaintances will come and go. Some friendships will last for a while others may be somewhat on the erratic side. You aren't possessive and indeed will tend to be amazingly open-handed with your possessions and your money. You might enjoy science, mystical subjects and delving into matters that cannot easily be explained. You will be inclined to join groups and organisations devoted to social and/or spiritual reform.

Ten of Spades: You have a strongly charitable side to your make-up. You're likely to be deeply sympathetic towards those in less fortunate circumstances. You have strong emotions and will be compassionate. You're fairly readily influenced by your feelings and emotions. You are highly imaginative and might find outlet for your wonderful imagination through art and creative past-times. You are psychic with natural healing ability.

Two of Diamonds: You are gentle, kind and affectionate. Feelings run deep and you tend to let your heart rule your head. You have many friends and this is thanks to your easy-going personality. You have a vivid imagination and a strong sense of spirituality. You are an empath: you can feel other people's emotions and their hurt as well as their happiness. You can put yourself in other people's shoes.

Three of Diamonds: You are highly sensitive to other people's needs and feelings and are likely to be generous to good causes. You are romantic and dreamy and love to live in your imagination. You are adaptable and are generally happy to go with the flow. You may have talent in writing, poetry, art and music. Sometimes, when you tune in carefully, you are sure you can hear the angels singing.

Four of Diamonds: You have energy and initiative. You take action when you feel it is required, in fact, you might find it hard to quell your excitable enthusiasm. You will have learned prudence through experience but there will always be a part of you that is ready for action. You have an outgoing nature and tend to be mainly orientated towards the outside world. Your interests will centre on things that are outside yourself for instance, other people, material realities and activities that take you out into the world.

Five of Diamonds: When you decide on something you get on with it, quickly. You hate waiting around for things to happen. You enjoy starting new projects and will take the initiative in all areas. You aren't a person to wait to hear what other people might think about it. You are generally confident and self-assured and you won't spend a lot of time wondering about whether or not you can do something. The best way to find out is to try and you will try anything once. There is a chance that you take on so much that despite your good intentions you don't always finish what you start.

Six of Diamonds: You are assertive and ambitious. You have high aspirations and ideals. You have creative ability including of the verbal kind. You can keep other people entertained with your interesting conversations. You also have the initiative to make some good accomplishments from your inspirations. You have a wonderful sense of humour and people feel uplifted in your company. Occasionally you will make a start on new ideas and inspirations with enthusiasm only to leave or forget about them as you move on to another subject so you never get around to actually finishing some projects.

Seven of Diamonds: You are fixed in opinion and aren't easily swayed once you make up your mind. There is a strong desire for stability and a need for regular routine as this makes you comfortable. When everything is normal and as it should be, you know where you stand. You are sensible and practical and have both feet planted firmly in the ground. You have a dislike of change unless change is essential. You would never make change for the sake of it. This goes for your possessions too. You wouldn't for instance just change your car in order to have the latest model. You value your possessions and will gather many around you through your life. This makes you feel secure. Regarding that car: you will be quite content with the one you have while it still works well!

Eight of Diamonds: You may be slow to come to opinions and slow to act but others should not be misled by this. You give all matters your full attention until you're confident you have grasped every detail and it is then that you will give a decision. Once you're sure of what you are doing other people will see a different side of you. Think of the speed a Spanish fighting bull can suddenly change direction. Even for that matter a heavy prize Hereford bull can give an awesome demonstration of turning ability, speed and acceleration. Once a decision is made you will act on it with confidence.

Nine of Diamonds: You make a thorough job of all that you do. You feel secure with a regular routine. Just as the year turns with the seasons, so do you roll through your regular routines. Some might think you plod through your days but what they may not see is how you work persistently and thoroughly. You work at your own pace so that at the end of every day everything will have been done properly. So each evening, you will be the one who can put up your feet and relax knowing all is in order while others who are less careful are still flitting about from here and there trying to rectify mistakes.

Ten of Diamonds: You have so many interests that sometimes it feels like there aren't enough hours in a day. You are friendly and easy-going and people enjoy your company. Your energy tends to be scattered too widely so that you might frequently over-extend yourself and in not knowing when to stop this can lead to nervous strain and exhaustion.

Two of Hearts: You are always on the go even when you are relaxing. You find it hard to sit still for more than a few minutes. Your mind is just as busy, always thinking, dreaming, discovering and delving into subjects that take your interest. You are inclined to be talkative but diplomatic too, with many interests including writing, travel and teaching ability.

Three of Hearts: You have a curious nature, interested in learning a little about a lot. You love reading, travel, mixing with other people and being on the go. There is a restlessness to your personality that keeps you going and you get bored very quickly if you stay in the same place or with the same subject for too long.

Four of Hearts: Emotions run deep and you are strongly in touch with your feelings. You are a loving and loyal friend. You take your relationships very seriously and your family mean the world to you. Four is a number of stability and your main source of stability lies within your home and family life. You hope to make a success of your life and your climb to success will be accompanied by a charming and sensitive manner with the basic iron fist well concealed by a velvet glove.

Five of Hearts: You have a deeply sensitive, caring and nurturing nature. Where your home and family matters are concerned, you will be reserved to the point of secrecy and you will take your family responsibilities seriously. Your home is a place to be closely guarded from prying eyes. It is or you wish it to be your safe haven where you can retreat from the outside world. You are highly intuitive and often remember your dreams.

Six of Hearts: You are emotional and imaginative and feel very deeply. You have a good memory and can sometimes tend to live in the past. You enjoy collecting items and many will have sentimental value to you. You can be relied on to keep a promise and friends value your loyalty. You have a sensitive and spiritual nature. Being by the sea, a river or stretch of water helps uplift you spiritually.

Seven of Hearts: You have a warm and enthusiastic nature with a natural ability to be a leader in your own sphere of operations. Home responsibilities will be taken seriously and in a caring manner. You can be slightly self-conscious and will occasionally sulk when things don't go your way. You are sensitive, generous and considerate overall. You are dependable and trustworthy as well as having a tendency to be fixed in your ways and resistant to change. You enjoy spending your hard earned money, after all, life is there to enjoy.

Eight of Hearts: You are positive and assertive with a drive to succeed. You have many friends and thrive when you are at the centre of all that is going on. You are a born optimist and have the ability to bring cheer into other people's lives. When you focus your energy towards creative outlets you can achieve wonderful works of art. You have a love of luxury and like to impress people with your expensive possessions.

Nine of Hearts: You are generous, loving and enthusiastic about your interests. You have natural leadership qualities and will do well in positions of authority. You tend to lead a luxurious lifestyle or would like to. You are creative and courageous and passionate. You are likely to have many friends and you will play a leading role in your social circle.

You have a lot of willpower and people look to you for guidance and for help, whenever they are in need. You can be a big spender and will splash out on anything from personal treats to luxury cruises and adventure holidays.

Ten of Hearts: You are practical and sensible with a lot of common sense. You try to be organised in all that you do and dislike being rushed. You prefer to get on with your work in your own way and in your own time. You are a perfectionist and will get annoyed with yourself if you don't meet the high standards you set for yourself. Other people know they can rely on you to fulfil your obligations and the number ten stands for completion ... you hate to leave loose-ends and like to finish anything you start.

Two of Clubs: You are curious and analytical and will spend hours studying subjects in order to dissect everything there is to know about them. You have a practical side and enjoy craftwork. You are intelligent and hard working and you prefer to work to set routines. You have high standards and believe that if a job is worth doing, it's worth doing properly. You like to feel useful and get a strong sense of satisfaction through being able to help other people.

Three of Clubs: You are careful and sensible, generally quiet and hard working. You keep your emotions to yourself and strive also to keep feelings under control. You are charming and polite and take a logical approach to life and life's challenges. This helps you tackle problems in a practical and analytical way. You are loyal to your friends and those you love and people can trust you never to let them down.

Four of Clubs: You have a kind and sensitive nature. Yours is a gentle personality and you would never deliberately hurt anyone. You would bend over backwards to please others. You are charming and creative and people enjoy your imaginative company. You appreciate art in all its forms. You tend to be laid-back and loving and you don't mind letting other people take the lead in your relationships. You're happy just to be in their company.

Five of Clubs: You are naturally diplomatic and charming. You can see all sides of a situation and you will find a way to get other people to see this too. You have a strong sense of justice and keen sense of wrong and right. You like to please people but should remember that it can do you good occasionally, to please yourself. You work well in partnerships and within groups.

Six of Clubs: When all aspects of your life are in harmony, you are at your happiest. You are charming and sensitive and you allow your head to have equal say to your heart. You are a good team player and communicate your thoughts clearly and honestly. You believe in honesty and have a strong sense of justice. You are a good listener and like to be in the company of other people. You prefer joint to solo activities.

Seven of Clubs: You are good at sensing other people's character almost as soon as you meet. You can see behind any façade straight into the person who is underneath. You live life in earnest and you are serious about anything you take on. That's why you will only commit yourself if you know you will be able to fulfil your obligations. You have intense feelings and will build a barrier around yourself to try to keep these under control and to prevent other people from intruding on your inner-life.

Eight of Clubs: You are a private person and very deep, spiritually and emotionally. You're quite hard to get to know and because you're always finding out new things about yourself, you might sometimes feel you don't know yourself. You will often delve deep inside to discover more about the inner-you. You're fascinated by the mysteries of life and probably believe in reincarnation. You have very deep feelings and are passionate about anything that grabs your interest.

Nine of Clubs: You like to feel useful and once you start on something you will persevere until it gets done, no matter how long it takes. You like to do a good job of anything you take on. You enjoy delving to the roots of any subject that captures your interest and you love uncovering hidden things. You are strongly intuitive and may have healing ability. Feelings run deep and your friends and loved ones will be familiar with your mood swings.

Ten of Clubs: You hate to be restricted in any way. Your love of freedom will often be expressed in an idealistic or even religious manner. Yours is a generally optimistic nature. You will be cheerful and optimistic, tolerant of others with a fair amount of self-confidence. You are enthusiastic and high spirited and have a wide range of experiences. You are a natural teacher and will prefer to show rather than tell.

Two of Spades: You love adventure and would feel bored if you were restricted to the same place for too long. You like to get out and about and discover what the rest of the world is getting up to. You constantly set new goals to work towards and these help keep you motivated. You like to feel you are constantly moving forward. You enjoy a challenge and will take the occasional risk to add a little excitement to life.

Three of Spades: You are optimistic and positive. You enjoy a challenge and would not be content in a routine day-to-day existence. You aren't good with repetition. You prefer to enjoy new and different experiences. You love travel and to discover more about other cultures and religions. You can be quite impulsive and quite enjoy taking the occasional risk.

Four of Spades: You take your responsibilities very seriously. Your sense of beauty is strong and you are likely to have artistic skills that you will use in a practical way. You have a strong rapport with nature and you tend to be careful and precise in all that you do. As well as being practical you are also sensitive. You don't like to admit to defeat and will persevere in your intentions until you get results.

(ix) Timing

You might use the following if you are trying to determine timing as shown by the cards:

Diamonds: Spring – March, April and May
Hearts: Summer – June, July and August
Clubs: Autumn – September, October and November
Spades: Winter – December, January and February

Ace of Diamonds would be at the very beginning of Spring (March)
Two of Diamonds: 1st to 10th March
Three of Diamonds: 11th to 20th March
Four of Diamonds: 21st to 30th March
Five of Diamonds: 1st to 10th April
Six of Diamonds: 11th to 20th April
Seven of Diamonds: 21st to 30th April
Eight of Diamonds: 1st to 10th May
Nine of Diamonds: 11th to 20th May
Ten of Diamonds: 21st to 30th May

Ace of Hearts would be at the very beginning of Summer (June)
Two of Hearts: 1st to 10th June
Three of Hearts: 11th to 20th June
Four of Hearts: 21st to 30th June
Five of Hearts: 1st to 10th July
Six of Hearts: 11th to 20th July
Seven of Hearts: 21st to 30th July
Eight of Hearts: 1st to 10th August
Nine of Hearts: 11th to 20th August
Ten of Hearts: 21st to 30th August

Ace of Clubs would be at the very beginning of Autumn (September)
Two of Clubs: 1st to 10th September
Three of Clubs: 11th to 20th September

Four of Clubs: 21st to 30th September
Five of Clubs: 1st to 10th October
Six of Clubs: 11th to 20th October
Seven of Clubs: 21st to 30th October
Eight of Clubs: 1st to 10th November
Nine of Clubs: 11th to 20th November
Ten of Clubs: 21st to 30th November

Ace of Spades would be at the very beginning of Winter
(December)
Two of Spades: 1st to 10th December
Three of Spades: 11th to 20th December
Four of Spades: 21st to 30th December
Five of Spades: 1st to 10th January--
Six of Spades: 11th to 20th January
Seven of Spades: 21st to 30th January
Eight of Spades: 1st to 10th February
Nine of Spades: 11th to 20th February
Ten of Spades: 21st to 30th February

(x) Example Readings

To help you understand how the cards are combined in a reading, here are examples of readings using some of the spreads in this book and the feedback after the reading.

Example of Reading Using Horseshoe Spread for Ashley

First Position: Matters of the past that relate to the present situation (ace of spades)

You feel clear in your mind about many aspects of your life, even matters which may have caused you confusion in the past. It's as if your mind is now clear of any mental fog that has been preventing you from seeing the situation as it is. You know when you make decisions, you will make the right ones for this present moment in time.

Second position: The present (Queen of Clubs)

You prefer to look on the bright side even when times are tough. You can lift people's spirits by bringing a touch of humour into even the most difficult situation. The Queen of Clubs puts you on centre stage. You could be in a position where others are gathering around you looking to you for support and guidance. You can offer praise to someone whose confidence needs a boost.

Third position: Developments in the near future (Two of Diamonds)

You would like to think you have the energy to fulfil all your goals and quickly but realistically you know you must take your time. Health wise, you need to take it slow and not push yourself past your limits. In a group setting you might sense some envy or hostility from someone and the best way to deal with this is not to say anything and be cautious when in this person's company.

Fourth position: Developments that may not be anticipated (Two of Clubs)

Your partner or a close friend could be arranging a surprise for you. This could be a romantic surprise or a small gift that will make your day.

Fifth position: People in your life who are linked to the present situation (Three of Clubs)

In your friendship and group relationships you are gaining more respect. People are starting to recognise and acknowledge your talents and you deserve the praise that is coming your way. Instead of just being in a group and watching from the side-lines, you are participating more now and you are getting a lot out of these endeavours.

Sixth position: Challenges and difficulties (Seven of Clubs)

You could find yourself in a position where you have to make a decision from several choices. This won't be easy. It may also be that there is someone in your life you aren't sure you can trust. If this person advises you on which choices to make, don't feel pushed into going along with their suggestions. Your decision should be your own.

Seventh position: Possible Outcomes (Eight of Clubs)

Movement is likely. You will feel you are moving forward in your life. This could involve you taking on more responsibilities or working towards new goals. Expect to make some positive accomplishments.

Together the Two of Diamonds and Two of Clubs put the spotlight on partnerships in your life and joint transactions and suggests these are an important area at this time.

Ashley's response to this reading: "OMGosh. Carole Anne you have blown me away! That is so accurate it's unbelievable." Later she got back to say her husband had arranged to have someone look after the children in the weekend so he could take her somewhere special.

Example Reading using Horseshoe Spread for Charlotte

First position: Matters of the past that relate to the present situation (Eight of Clubs)
You've just been through a deeply emotional time and you are likely to still be feeling the fall-out of this experience in the present. Emotional wounds are still very raw. Just like a physical wound that is healed and can leave a scar in its place, emotional scars too will remain and your memory will sometimes remind you of the experiences that caused this wound. Out of this you will learn more about yourself and your strengths. A relationship or situation did not pan out as you expected however emotional and spiritual experiences such as this one can help transform pain into spiritual growth and higher levels of emotional maturity.

Second position: The present (Nine of Clubs)
You have been through a lot lately. – Challenges and some soul-searching too. You still haven't quite been able to push all difficulties or confusion behind you. It will take time for emotional wounds to heal.
You're putting on a brave face in front of the world but underneath you don't feel so confident. In fact sometimes you just want to shut the door on the world and hide in a corner where no-one can see you. You will however find the strength within to help you emerge from this situation with your head held high.

Third position: Developments in the near future (Nine of Spades)
A stressful situation, your health or a situation that has causing you some anxiety is still holding you back. Even though you don't want it to.

You're determined to move forward but your current mind-set prevents you from being able to do this. Someone may have been playing mind-games with you or they've been using emotional blackmail in order to try to get their own way. Don't doubt yourself no matter what anyone else tells you. You will pull yourself out of this situation and you will be stronger and more confident as a result.

Fourth position: Developments that may not be anticipated (Nine of Diamonds)

A new career opportunity could present itself and you will not have been anticipating this. It could be that you will receive some kind of bonus or an offer that will make a difference to your finances. This might also help you put some home redecorating plans into action or buy items for your home and garden that you've been thinking about lately.

Fifth position: People in the sitter's life who are linked to the present situation (Jack of Clubs)

A dark haired young man in your life is making his presence felt very strongly. Also if you're wondering whether you will be able to move forward it could be that a sudden and spontaneous decision or offer will help you move onto what you feel is the right path for you.

Sixth position: Challenges and difficulties (Three of Spades)

There is a lot of emotion in your reading and something you are going through will have your emotions whirling around very strongly. Will you ever find true happiness you may be wondering? You will overcome current challenges and you will be able to put a past difficult situation behind you as new doors will be opening up for you taking you to a happier place.

Seventh position: Possible outcomes (Three of Diamonds)

Correspondence linked with legal or financial matters will mark the beginning of a new phase in life. You will be laying down the foundations of a new future for yourself. There may be a chance to take on some training to do with your job. You will find yourself feeling more optimistic about your future.

You had two cards in your spread with the number three and three cards with the number nine. This suggests that some aspects of your life are coming to a completion ready for new beginnings and there will be something to celebrate soon.

Charlotte's Response to her reading: "Thank you sooo much! This is an amazing reading! The past few years have been an emotional roller coaster for sure. I'm still working through a lot of life issues. The past few months have been exceptionally trying with a new relationship, spiritual events, and just an insane amount of change taking place in my life. The stressful situation coming could be so many things. A lot is up in the air right now with finance, family, and my home. It does have my attention and I'm sure it will get more crazy and stressful before it gets better but I have total faith it will all works itself out in the end. As far as work: a bonus or promotion would be welcome for sure!
   The dark haired man is probably my ex. I have been having a lot of dreams about him. He is also the cause of a lot of those scars you speak of. I feel I am going to bump into him somehow or he will be attempting to contact me soon. That usually happens when I find him on my mind a lot. This is such a wonderful and detailed reading! And form playing cards! Amazing."

Example of a Five Card Situation Spread for Samantha

1 The situation to be dealt with (10 Clubs)

It is likely the situation that's on your mind will be of an official nature. This will involve meetings or an interview-type situation. Although other cards need to be considered there is a strong possibility that you will be happy with the eventual results.

2 Your task in order to resolve this situation (10 Spades)

You have been through or are going through a number of challenges in having to deal with this issue. You wonder if it will ever end and will things improve. Sometimes you wish you had more control or it feels as if someone else is trying to control the situation but you are not powerless in this and you are able to push for what you want or feel is right. You need to be firm with yourself when dealing with this as you have a tendency to make sacrifices to keep other people happy. You are ready now to resolve difficult situations as the pressure is becoming too much for you and you are ready to resolve matters and put it all behind you.

3 Issues you are not aware of (Queen Diamonds)

There is someone who is wanting to protect you ... a strong motherly influence is with you that you may not have realised or aren't aware of. This is a person or someone in spirit who is helping to guide and support you. Or this could be a friend who understands what you are going through and she will be such a strong support if you need confidential advice.

4 Possible solution (Two of Spades)

Trust your intuition rather than listen to what other people are telling you. Confusion can result from paying too much attention to what others want and forgetting about your own needs. Take a deep breath and remind yourself that you are strong and you can trust your intuition. Don't keep telling yourself you're going to make the wrong decision. Have faith that you are making the right ones.

5 Conclusion/outcome (Ace of Clubs)

Because an Ace has fallen in the outcome placement of your spread this suggests that a successful conclusion to this situation will lead to new beginnings. You will be ready to take new directions in relation to your own goals and ambitions. There will be such a relief when this situation that is hanging over you is over that you will feel a gush of energy for something new. You could be drawn to an exciting new hobby or interest that will require both energy and creativity.

Samantha's response to her reading: "Thank you so much. This all makes perfect sense and seems to relate to my folks estate which has been a huge burden for two years. I do need to listen and trust myself more on all matters and I'm really looking forward to starting something new! My mom is in spirit, and I know she would help if she could. I also have a wonderful friend who is always there for me."

Example of a Five Card Past and Future Spread for Barbara

1 Past (Eight of Clubs)

You've been through quite some emotional or spiritual turmoil. You haven't been standing still. I feel you've been putting a lot of emotion and energy into your aims and this has helped steer you away from difficulties of the past or issues that have been holding you back. A situation in your life, or some hopes you had, didn't quite turn out as expected and there may have been some emotional or spiritual confusion. But you are moving away from all of this now.

2 Present (Nine of Clubs)

You're making a great effort to keep on top of everything and to please other people. You're putting so much energy into your current projects, hoping that this will be a good investment for your future. It gets tiring though and often it feels like a lot of effort for little recompense. There are moments you just want to shut the door on the rest of the world and hide away but you know this won't get you to the place you want to be. You will find the strength and determination to continue and you should feel proud of yourself for your achievements so far. Keep reminding yourself, as you probably already do, that hard work will bring its just rewards.

3 Hidden influences (Ten of Clubs)

You're almost too nervous to think that your hopes will be realised and yet positive thinking will attract positive things your way. Happiness is in your cards and contentment in relationships. Some of your dreams are starting to be realised.

4 New Possibilities (Jack of Clubs)

There may be opportunities in the future linked with a dark haired young man and this is someone who can be trusted. Your intuition will guide you to the right paths. A sudden opportunity or a spontaneous offer someone gives you could seem like too good a chance to miss.

5 Outcome (Queen of Spades)

You are ambitious and you push yourself very hard. You have high expectations from yourself. It could be this keeps you a little rigid in your thinking. It might help to think outside the box, to experiment in new areas, to try interests that are new to you. As you move forward, so your interests and abilities will expand, bringing new possibilities into your future.

The Two of Clubs fell out while I was shuffling so this card wanted to make itself felt to you. In some areas of your life you might feel as if you haven't quite had a chance to prepare for what has occurred. Some challenges may therefore relate to what has been agreed on in the past when certain matters have been overlooked or weren't considered at the time. These obstacles can be easily overcome. Also I feel an offer or opportunity that comes your way will take you completely by surprise.

Barbara's response to her reading: "You just narrated my recent current situation Carole Anne ... awesome!"

Final Note:

In all methods of fortune telling, remember that the associations of each cards is subjective and each card can mean different things to different people. Nothing is "written in stone". Also when reading the cards, they should be weighed up with the other cards that have appeared in a spread.

Acknowledgement:

While some names have been changed to protect privacy, to those who allowed me to share their readings in this book: Thank you.

If you enjoyed this book, further books by this author can be found at:
Amazon.co.uk – Carole Somerville
Amazon.com – Carole Somerville

Printed in the USA
CPSIA information can be obtained
at www.ICGtesting.com
LVHW051921121023
760979LV00008B/242